RACE CARS

by Darlene R. Stille

Content Adviser: Professor Sherry L. Field,
Department of Social Science Education, College of Education,
The University of Georgia
Reading Adviser: Dr. Linda D. Labbo,
Department of Reading Education, College of Education,
The University of Georgia

Compass Point Books

Minneapolis, Minnesota

Compass Point Books
3722 West 50th Street, #115
Minneapolis, MN 55410

Visit Compass Point Books on the Internet at *www.compasspointbooks.com* or e-mail your request to *custserv@compasspointbooks.com*

Photographs ©: Allsport Photography, cover, 4–5, 6–7, 8–9, 12–13, 22–23, 24–25, 26; SportsChrome USA/Brian Spurlock, 1; Louise A. Noeth, 10–11, 14–15, 20–21; Unicorn Stock Photos/Russell R. Grundke, 16–17; Unicorn Stock Photos/Mark Romesser, 18–19.

Editors: E. Russell Primm and Emily J. Dolbear
Photo Researcher: Svetlana Zhurkina
Photo Selector: Melissa Voda
Designer: Melissa Voda

Library of Congress Cataloging-in-Publication Data
Stille, Darlene R.
   Race cars / by Darlene R. Stille.
     p. cm. — (Transportation)
   Includes bibliographical references and index.
   ISBN 0-7565-0149-0 (hardcover, library binding)
     1. Automobiles, Racing—Juvenile literature. [1. Automobiles, Racing. 2. Automobile racing.] I. Title.
TL236 .S746 2001
629.228—dc21 2001001447

J
629.228
STI
c.1

5-09

© 2002 by Compass Point Books

Table of Contents

The Race Begins

The green flag waves. The race starts. See the cars zoom by. What an exciting sport! Have you been to an auto race? Have you watched race cars on television?

There are many kinds of cars and races. What kind of race would you like to see? What kind of race car would you like to drive?

Racing Formula One and Indy Cars

Formula One and Indy cars are made for racing. They are not like the cars on the streets. They have only one seat. They have no roof. There are no fenders over the wheels. The engine is in the back.

The body of a Formula One or an Indy car is shaped like a tube. There are short "wings" on the front and back. These help hold the car on the ground when it is going fast.

7

Racing a Stock Car

Stock cars are made from standard American-made automobiles. Stock cars are painted bright colors. Powerful engines make the cars go fast.

People drive stock cars in NASCAR races. NASCAR stands for National Association for Stock Car Auto Racing. The Daytona 500 in Florida is a famous NASCAR race.

Racing a Sports Car

A classic sports car has only two seats and two doors. One famous American sports car is the Chevrolet Corvette.

Some regular sports cars are also racing sports cars. Other sports cars are made just for racing.

Drag Racing

All kinds of cars race on drag strips. A drag strip is a straight paved track. It is usually 1/4 mile (0.4 kilometers) long—or about two city blocks. Drag races are short and fast. Some cars go so fast that they have a parachute in the rear to slow them down.

A pro stock car is a drag-racing car made from a regular car. Dragsters, however, are cars made just for drag racing. Dragsters have one seat, huge back tires, and tiny front tires. Dragsters are also called top fuel cars.

Racing a Hot Rod

Hot rods are another kind of drag-racing car. A hot rod is made from an old car. You take off the hood and fenders. You then put in a powerful engine.

The first hot rods were made in the 1930s. Some people make hot rods as a hobby.

The Soap Box Derby

Boys and girls can drive in some races. They drive soap-box racers. A soap-box racer does not have an engine. It glides up and down hills.

Boys and girls make their own soap-box racers from kits. First, they race in their own area. Winners go on to the Soap Box Derby in Akron, Ohio.

Racing a Kart

Some boys and girls start racing karts when they are eight or nine years old. A kart has an engine.

Karts have a simple frame. The frame includes one seat, a small engine, and the wheels. Kart races are shorter than automobile races.

Racing a Midget Car

A midget car is a small race car with a modified small engine. It is bigger than a kart and does not have a roof or fenders.

A quarter midget is one-fourth the size of a midget car. Boys and girls from five to sixteen years old race quarter midgets. Many grown-up race drivers once competed in quarter midgets or karts.

In the Race

Let's drive in a road race. You can drive a Formula One car or a sports car on a hilly road with many sharp turns.

Let's drive on an oval-shaped track. It has straight parts and curved parts. You can drive a stock car, Indy car, midget, or kart on a track.

Let's drive part of the race on an oval track and part of the race on a road. You drive a sports car in this kind of race.

Meet the Pit Crew

You are in a close race. Suddenly you get a flat tire. You stop at a place called the pit. Your pit crew runs out. They are all auto mechanics. They work very fast.

Count to ten. That's about how long it takes the pit crew to change your tire! You are back in the race again.

Winning the Race

The race is over. The crowd cheers for the winning driver.

Race-car drivers work hard to win. They take lessons at race-car driving school. They practice driving. They learn about safety. They wear a helmet and fireproof clothing in case of a crash. They learn that the driver is part of a team. The car builder and the pit crew are also part of the team. The team works together to win—and to finish the race safely.

Glossary

association—an organization, club, or society

fenders—metal covers that protect wheels from damage and reduce splashing

glides—moves smoothly and easily

paved—covered with concrete or asphalt

pit—an area alongside a racetrack used for fixing a car during a race

Did You Know?

NASCAR was started in 1948.

In February 1999, Tory Schumacher became the first drag-car racer to reach a speed of 330 miles (530 kilometers) per hour.

The first Indianapolis 500 race was held in 1911 and was won by Ray Harroun. His average speed was 75 miles (120 kilometers) per hour.

Indy car fuel cells (gas tanks) hold 40 gallons (151 liters). They can be filled in about 10 seconds during a pit stop.

Want to Know More?

At the Library

Bingham, Caroline, and Deni Brown. *Mighty Machines: Race Car*. New York: DK Publishing, 1996.

Rex, Michael. *My Race Car*. New York: Henry Holt, 2000.

Stephenson, Sal. *Race Cars*. Mankato, Minn.: Capstone Press, 1991.

Carey, Craig Robert. *Race Cars*. New York: Golden Books, Inc., 2001.

Cook, Nick. *The World's Fastest Cars*. Mankato, Minn.: Capstone Press, 2000.

On the Web

PBS Online: Race Cars

http://www.pbs.org/tal/racecars/build.html

To build your own race car online

NASCAR

http://www.nascar.com

To view NASCAR's official web site with links, photos, and information

The Soap Box Derby

http://www.soapboxderby.org

For information on past winners, a gallery of photos, a derby simulation, and much more

Formula One Racing

http://www.formula1.com/

To play games, view photos, check headlines, and much more

Through the Mail

ESPN

ESPN Plaza
Bristol, CT 06010
For more information on race cars and all types of motor sports

On the Road

Indianapolis Motor Speedway

4790 West 16th Street
Indianapolis, IN 46222
The Indianapolis 500 is held in early May at the Indianapolis Motor Speedway.

Index

About the Author

Darlene R. Stille is a science editor and writer. She has lived in Chicago, Illinois, all her life. When she was in high school, she fell in love with science. While attending the University of Illinois, she discovered that she also enjoyed writing. Today she feels fortunate to have a career that allows her to pursue both her interests. Darlene R. Stille has written more than thirty books for young people.